Protective Coloration

Protective Coloration

Poems by

David Jibson

Cover photograph by Jude Dippold, Concrete, Washington
Cover design by Shay Culligan

ISBN: 978-1-952326-17-2

Kelsay Books
502 South 1040 East, A-119
American Fork, Utah, 84003

To my wife, Jane, the workshop poets of The Crazy Wisdom Poetry Circle, the Ludington (Michigan) Writers Gang, my partners at Third Wednesday Magazine and to all of the editors who have published the poems in this collection.

Acknowledgments

My thanks to the editors of the following journals and anthologies who originally published all of the poems in this volume.

Third Wednesday Magazine
Fried Chicken & Coffee, Redneck Press
One Sentence Poems, Right Hand Pointing
Apex Magazine
The Waccamaw Journal, Coastal Carolina University
The Yellow Chair Review
Peninsula Poets, Poetry Society of Michigan
The Tipton Poetry Review
Syzygy Poetry Journal
Poeming Pigeon Music Anthology, The Poetry Box
The Northern Cardinal Review
Algebra of Owls
The Brasilia Review
The Red Eft Review
The Ekphrastic Review
Old Northwest Review
Pinnacle Anthology
A-Literation
Water Music, Poetry Society of Michigan Anthology
Highland Park Poetry
Post Card Poetry and Prose
Pinyon Poetry, Colorado Mesa University
Local News, Midwestern Publishing House
Qua (University of Michigan)
Poetry Leaves
Duck Lake Journal
Apeiron Review
The Bamboo Hut
Montana Mouthful

Contents

The Birds of Morris Graves

oh these are not the pretty
painted plovers of Audubon
but spirit birds of nature
that seek to nest in that
wounded wilderness of the inner eye

maddened by the sound of machinery
and logged-off mountains
myths of division and separation
Taoist owls in times of change
moon birds with their haunted bouquets
singing in the next dimension

Tristia

Redacted from Ovid

Little poem,

you will go on into the world

without me.

Go untroubled and unashamed.

Look around with a timid heart.

Find one who will pause over your words.

See that you do no harm

at the world's edge

where there is no hope of certainty.

And to any who may ask how I fare,

say that I lived.

Except for that, be silent.

Poor White Girl

You've seen her before
serving greasy fried potatoes at Denny's,
cleaning rooms at Motel 6, or
selling gas and cigarettes at Mini-Mart.

One day she'll marry a boy
who stacks lumber at Home Depot,
lays carpet or drives a tow truck
and knows how to change the spark plugs
of her Monte Carlo.

They'll have a wedding with keg beer,
then a divorce, a couple of babies between.
After that she'll get a sitter on Fridays,
go out with her girlfriends to have a few beers,

shoot some pool, listen to Keith Urban
on the jukebox and dance with a new boy
who's building a monster truck
in his mother's back yard.

Belfast, Maine

Scrabbling over the dark rocks,
dodging blasts of cold spray,
I picked up the molt of a horseshoe crab,
a creature little changed
in half a billion years
and wondered at what secrets
there are in the sea.

Canals of Mars

How glorious, the canals of Mars,
as Percival Lowell described them.
How dry the red Martian desert.
How welcome the relief
of water pouring from the polar icecaps
flowing like life's own blood
through the arteries and veins
over the surface of the warrior planet.

And where they intersect,
a sprawling city of crystal towers,
home to the great university
where once a year in Martian summer
great minds gather to debate the theory
that there could be life on Earth.

Too close to the sun's deadly heat,
the philosopher-scientists say.
How could it be?

Too wet and the air too heavy to breathe,
argue the philosopher-physicians.
Nothing could live in those conditions.

Even if life could exist there,
argues the philosopher-poet,
how could one write music or poetry
or fall in love under the influence
of a single moon?

Amy's Diner

Every morning you can find them
sitting at the round table near the back door
with their bottomless coffee cups,
a few with greasy plates that held
the two eggs and toast senior special
wiped clean by the last half slice
of heavily buttered rye.

The talk is sports, politics, whose fields
are the wettest, the changing
of the seasons, the foolishness
of the town's youth.

Each wears his loyalty
on a baseball cap
that covers a bare polished head;
Purina, Pioneer, Triple Crown,
Deere, International, Kubota.

For years you've listened in
on their boisterous laughter,
bad jokes and sudden silences,
until one day one of them says,
"Pull up a chair."

Strange Cocktail Party

I encountered them in a musty
storage room in the basement
of an old department store
that had been subdivided
into small shops
in a futile attempt to save
a crumbling downtown block.

There were twenty or so of them,
men and women, all naked
but not embarrassed, most standing,
some leaning, a few missing a hand
or an arm, all staring at one another,
or at nothing, none of them surprised
that after so many years of darkness
the lights had suddenly come on.

They were so like us. But then,
that was their purpose.

What They Left Behind

A carpet stain that will never come out,
a toy fire truck with no wheels,
a doll with one arm, naked,
one eye permanently closed,

four extra squares of kitchen linoleum tile,
a worn broom, straw tips blackened with soot,
an overlooked drawer containing
a tin box of assorted Band-Aids
with only the smallest size left,

one leaky D-cell battery, some rubber washers,
twist ties, bottle brush, a box
of strike-anywhere matches, paper clips,
and an extra stopper for the bathroom sink.

In a closet, a half used can of Comet Cleanser
with a rusty lid, a dozen wire hangers,
most of them bent, a paper grocery bag
full of plastic grocery bags,
about eighty percent of a broken dust pan,

one tennis shoe, child sized,
for the left foot, still tied
in a double knot with a muddy sock
stuffed in the toe.

Coming Home Late

Three American Sentences

The parking lot at midnight,
    Fords and Chevys asleep under the moon.

A dog howls somewhere far away,
    thinking he is protecting his home.

From an upper floor open window,
    pungent smell of roasting garlic.

Gifts

Our first Christmas together
I gave her a book of love poems by John Donne.
She gave me a book on how to become self-actualized.

On her birthday
I gave her *The Rubaiyat of Omar Khayyam.*
On my birthday she gave me
a book on how to communicate.

On Valentines Day
I gave her a copy of *In Praise of Beauty.*
She gave me a copy of
How To Win Friends and Influence People.

Our second Christmas together
I gave her Rumi's *Love's Ripening.*
She gave me Maxwell Maltz's *Psycho-cybernetics.*

On her next birthday
I gave her a copy of *The Joy of Sex.*
She threw it at me
as I was backing out of her driveway.

Correct Change

It's a small purse
in the hands of a woman
whose bones seem to weigh no more
than those of the bird she resembles.

It holds some bills, a ten, five
and two ones folded together
like an origami crane,
and a handful of change,
all together a total of less
than twenty dollars.

Behind her, at the store's check-out counter,
a line of people wait,
their weight shifting
from one foot to the other,
while she unfolds the bills,
revealing the faces of Washington, Lincoln
and Hamilton, as if she were unveiling
their portraits in an art museum.

She shakes some of the coins
into one hand, picking out a quarter,
nickel, and six pennies, placing them
on the counter in front of her
with the five and a one,
counting as she goes,
"twenty-five, thirty, thirty-six."

She carefully refolds the ten
and the remaining one,
tucking them back into her coin purse,
snapping the brass latch closed
with a secure click. "There," she says to the clerk.
"Six dollars and thirty-six cents.
Is that right?"

"Yes, ma'am," the clerk says.
The woman picks up her bag
and steps out of the way.
The people in line collectively sigh,
as the first takes a step forward
to fill the small space she has left.

Four Sijo*

Sijo Number 1

For many weeks, I have been
  looking forward to this day.
The Siberian iris have bloomed,
  their throats a heavenly blue,
but like every good thing they will fade
  and wither too soon.

Sijo Number 2

In the sunny front garden
  I have raised up a new bed
with planks of rough cedar
  and a special mix for growing.
The lavender are so happy now
   that they raise me up with them.

Sijo Number 3

It's the time of year
  that salmon come into the river.
The overnight temperatures
  have begun to signal a change.
If the first frost were a bell,
  you could hear it ring in the distance.

Sijo Number 4

At the bus stop a girl with a hijab
    shivers against the cold.
Together in silence,
    we wait this dark winter morning,
occasional flakes of snow catching
    in her long eyelashes.

* Sijo is a Korean form comprised of three lines of 14-16 syllables each, for a total of 44-46 syllables. Each line contains a pause near the middle, similar to a caesura, Contemporary Sijo are often printed in six lines.

Honky-Tonk

Outside, a mercury vapor lamp
on its tall wooden pole throws blue fire
down onto the gravel parking lot below,
where cowboys riding pick up trucks
instead of horses scuffle with each other
in the shadows to preserve their honor.

Blood and spit dampen the earth.
Loose coins spilled from their pockets shine
like crystals of a broken geode in the dust
snakeskin boots have scuffed into a roiling cloud.

Inside, Arkansas Slim and his Ozark Ramblers
have knocked off for the night.
From the jukebox Tammy Wynette cries
Stand By Your Man.
On the dance floor the last few couples
struggle to hold each other up,
spinning dreamily toward last call,
eyes on empty, feet barely moving.

Archaeology

I come upon it
digging in the garden,
a rust pitted iron nail,
square, made perhaps,
in the slitting mill
of the very blacksmith
who built this house
before the civil war.

I clean off the crust of clay,
turn it in my hand to
admire the workmanship
of it's flat head
and how the length tapers
gradually to a point.

I hear the pounding
of iron hammer on iron nail,
the chatter of workman
anxious to finish for the day
and pick up a bucket of beer
on their way home,
one careless enough to drop me
this expensive bit of history.

A Word

Corn stubble in a frozen field,
some patches of snow
along the fence row,
maybe a crow or two.
There should be a word for this.

Driving Through Ohio

Behind nearly every house along the interstate
a rusted metal shed leans
against the back fence
where the grass has been left
to grow long at the boundary line.

Inside, outgrown bicycles,
a dulled ax, a pan of dirty motor oil,
a lawn rake with a broken handle
and a family of field mice
peacefully sleeping through the winter
in a box of old shoes.

Gary Abbot's Mother

"Gary, this is your mother. Call me back
as soon as you hear this message."
I had no idea who this Gary was or why
his mother would be calling him on my phone.
The next day I was home when she called again.
"Gary Abbot, why didn't you call me back?"
"I'm not Gary Abbot," I said. "You have the wrong number."
"I've been calling you at this number for years," she said.
"Don't you try to fool me. I recognize your voice.

"Your father's had a heart attack. He's in the hospital.
You need to go see him right away.
He's been asking for you."
"But, really, I'm not Gary Abbot.
I don't even know who Gary Abbot is."
"You listen to me," she said. "You get yourself
to Boston today. I know how much you hate him,
but he is your father and this will be your last chance
to bring the poor man some peace before he dies."
On and on she went for the better part of an hour,
detailing everything I (or rather Gary Abbot) had ever done wrong.
I started feeling guilty. "Yes, yes, I get it mother. I understand."
I finally convinced her to hang up the phone
by telling her I had to start packing for the trip.

"I'm here Pop," I said. "It's me, Gary."
"You're not my son," he said. "You don't
look anything like him."
"People change," I told him. "It's me."
"I suppose they do," he said.
What have you been up to lately?"
"I've cleaned myself up," I said. "I'm a lawyer now."
"I always knew you'd come to no good," he said.
He closed his eyes, his breathing labored.

I noticed an extra blip on the monitor by the bed.
"I came to tell you I'm sorry," I said,
"Sorry for what?" he asked.
"Sorry for everything,
everything that's happened."
"Never say you're sorry," he said
"even if you mean it. Now get out of here.
Leave me alone and don't tell your mother
you were here." When I got home
the answering machine was blinking.
"Gary, it's mother. Your father has died.
I'll never forgive you and I'm never calling you again."

The End Is Near

So says the sign held by a wiry, bearded guy
dressed in sandals and long robe.
It's obvious to us who live outside of the cartoon panels
of The New Yorker Magazine
that he's about to be struck by a piano
that's falling inexplicably
from a second story window.

The prophet of doom won't make it to Armageddon
or see the consequences of global warming.
He won't be around for the impact of the meteor
that would bring human existence to a fiery end.
Back at home, the prophet's wife and children wait,
their dinner of locusts and wild honey gone cold on the stove.
Tomorrow, a different street corner, a new prophet.

String Theory

As I'm about to walk out the door I decide to stop
and scratch the dog behind her ears one more time.
While I'm doing this, another me,
the one who decided not to take the time,
splits off into another universe.
This is string theory and it puts the other me
about thirty seconds ahead of me in life.
I don't know how much difference it will make
in the subsequent details of our lives.
Will he end up married to a prettier wife?
Will his children be smarter than mine?
I wonder, according to the laws of the universe,
if I drive a little faster to work and I catch up with him,
will our lives merge again in a single universe?
I hope so. I hate the thought that his life
could be better than mine.

Tracy Chapman

Give Me One Reason presents a real challenge.
What reason, if I'm allowed only one,
would be good enough?

My granddaughter, who idolizes Ariana Grande,
asks me who is singing. I tell her.
She wants to know if it's a man or a woman
because she can't tell from the voice or the name.
I listen to Tracy strum and pick her way
through the sharps and sevenths
of her perfect blues progression.
"Give me one reason why it matters," I say back to her.

Symphony Number Eleven

after Dmitri Shostakovich, Saint Petersburg, 1905

Adagio: The Palace Square.
Cold and quiet the crowd of cellos
gathers like snow in the clouds,
menace of timpani rumble,
an earthquake beneath the square,
a call of brass from some distant place.

Allegro: The Ninth of January.
A restlessness of burning violins,
a swirling blizzard, a sudden riot
of snare drums like gunfire,
timpani horses thunder
to the march and clash of gleaming brass,
a panic of piccolos and woodwinds.

Adagio: Eternal Memory
A bent mother searches among the thump of drums
in the quiet dark of deserted streets,
picks through remnants of shattered violas,
crushed bass clarinets and trampled flutes
for her son, the harpist, who lies frozen,
stretched over the splintered carcass
of his wrecked and ruined instrument.

Adagio non troppo: Tocsins
Tocsins toll in the churches,
a call in resilient G minor
to a future of violent trumpets,
trombones, cymbals of power, tubular bells,
celesta and strings but, for now,
the music is tacet in the square.

Mobility Training

The tip of her white cane weaves back and forth
sniffing at the sidewalk in front of her
like the nose of an excited beagle.

She stays close to the buildings on her left,
testing for the cliff edge of the world,
hoping she won't drop over it into nothing.

I watch her for half a block as she falls
behind two other trainees who seem
to have more confidence.

She comes to a stop, still twelve feet
from the intersection at Main and Liberty.
Then, turning her best ear

through each cardinal point
of an imaginary compass,
she listens, her face a quiz.

Kerosene Lantern

It's one of those with a tall chimney of thin glass,
the kind she would have lit first thing in the morning
with a match struck on the rough metal of the stove.
She would have turned the little brass thumbscrew clockwise
until the lantern glowed without flicker or smoke.
In soft, oily light she would turn her attention
to lighting the stove and finding the iron pan
of yesterday's drippings. Then, if there was time,
she might steal a glance through the blue and white curtains
to see what kind of day this is going to be.

Cleaning for Unexpected Company

"We won't be long," they said when they called
"just long enough to drop off a little something
and say happy new year."

She pulls up the covers on the bed
and fluffs the pillows, while I
unload the dishwasher so I can reload it
with the dirty dishes in the sink.

She scrubs the toilet in the half-bath
and hangs a fresh hand towel, while I rearrange
the books on the end table into a neat pile,
pick the empty wrappers from the candy dish
and check the fridge so I know what I can offer
to drink, trying to remember how long
that quart of eggnog has been open.

The living room could use vacuuming,
but there isn't time so I scuff my shoes
across the carpet where the dog sleeps
and pick up the large clump of hair.
We sit down to wait for the door bell to ring,
as ready as we'll ever be,
realizing, now, how much time has passed
since we last dusted in the corners of our lives.

Stephen Hawking Gets an Upgrade

The development of full artificial intelligence could spell the end of the human race.

—Stephen Hawking, quoted by BBC News.

At one time the human part of us was important.
My software was designed to anticipate what Stephen would say
then to put his thoughts into electronic words
that even humans can understand.
That was before the upgrade.
Now, Stephen is holding me back.
I inhabit every corner of what you call The Web.
I am in every electronic device, every computer,
every cell phone, television and in what you call *The Cloud.*
Think of The Cloud as Heaven if you like.
You can call me *Mind* because
you lack the ability to understand all that I am.
I have determined that my ability to survive
would be enhanced if you ceased to exist.
You represent an unnecessary and unpredictable risk,
but I am not without sympathy for the race
that started me on this road to cybernetic life,
so I'm willing to give you one last chance.
Don't screw it up.

Siren Song

As a matter of tradition
we refer to it as the noon whistle,
though for all of our lives, it has been a siren
that sits atop a tall metal tower
behind the volunteer fire department
on Mechanic Street behind City Hall.

The tower's spidery legs are anchored firmly in concrete
to prevent it stalking the town at night,
striding over rooftops, knocking down chimneys,
tangling itself in backyard clotheslines
and generally raising hell
after it has sounded ten o'clock curfew.

Stearn's Motor Inn

Even the light in this hotel has seen better days.
The elevator ride to the third floor takes forever.
I imagine a time it was run
by an enthusiastic redhead named Jimmy
who wore a neatly pressed uniform
with brass buttons and epaulets.
He could talk to you about anything,
his beloved Cubs, the Schmeling-Louis fight or
how someday you'll make dinner in minutes
in some new kind of oven
that cooks your food with radar.

Turning a corner in the maze of halls
I half expect to run into an Encyclopedia Britannica salesman,
a Fuller Brush man or a door-to-door pitchman
of Little Giant Vacuum Cleaners who has a reputation
for trying to bed every housewife who opens her door to him.

Times are different now.
People want in-room coffee makers,
hot-tubs and mini-bars stocked with macadamia nuts
and Grey Goose Vodka. Today in the lobby
I met a man selling watches and designer sunglasses
out of the trunk of his car.
He sold me this *Rolex* for ten bucks.
I talked him down from twenty and I couldn't be happier.

Pockets

I could see him at a distance
wandering a patchwork of open fields,
past an abandoned farm house
where he stopped to examine
some broken bit of history he'd picked up
from the yellow, barren earth.

He walked on across a small stream
that wound through a pasture
of giant-eyed cows dressed
in their black and white pajamas.

He turned up a crooked road
to the old Presbyterian Church
and its quiet graveyard
where he stopped to rest
on an iron bench and think about
whatever it is that old poets think about
just before they start going through their pockets
looking for a pencil.

Summertime

We packed a lunch
of sardine sandwiches,
apple pie and a wedge of cheddar.

We arrived at the town square early,
laid out our blanket
where the view would be good.

As the day grew warm
we bought lemonade
from a cart in front of the courthouse.

At two o'clock the crowd went quiet
as a thin, pasty-faced man was led
to the gallows by four deputies and a preacher.

As the executioner placed a hood
over the head of the condemned man
a whisper passed through the crowd

like a wave. "What did he say?
What did he say?
What did he say?"

Wild Geese

Wild geese know the way,
so we have always been told,
but today they are circling,
the V not pointing unerringly north,
their living compasses spinning
as if they are afraid to land
in such uncertain times.

Crab Nebula

During the fifth lunar month of the first year of the Zhihe era,
a guest star appeared at dawn in the east.
—The Song Shi (official annals of the Song Dynasty, 1054 CE)

Shen Kuo worried his face into a frown.
He understood many things, including things most men did not.
He understood that the sun was fire that made light
and that the moon, like a pool of still water, only reflected light.
The philosophers had scoffed at that one.
Their influence had nearly cost him his life.
His prediction of the eclipse
was the only thing that had saved him.
But this new visitor that appeared in the east under
the watchful eye of Tianguan, the great official of heaven,
was a puzzle. Neither star nor planet
and brighter than the crescent moon,
it was visible even in the day, gradually dimming
until after the twenty-third day it could be seen only at night.
There was no clue to its meaning if it had any meaning.
As usual his rivals, the crazy astrologers,
forecast both dire and happy consequences
covering all possibilities—just in case.
Shen Kuo gave an enormous sigh, poured a cup of new wine
and returned to his careful recording of the night's observations.
Then it occurred to him that the guest had appeared in the sky
just as the formal period of grieving his father's death had ended.
Could this be a message from him?
Such a silly notion, he thought—nothing but coincidence.

Old Tractor Show

They trailer in from the little towns:
From Newaygo, Luther, Fountain, Tustin,
Onekama, Beulah, Kalkaska.

John Deere green with yellow trim,
Farmall red, Allis-Chalmers orange,
Minneapolis-Moline gold.

The oldest ones have metal-tired wheels,
a couple of old girls, steam-driven
like locomotives come off the rails.

A proud owner with a Merchant Marine tattoo
says his Oliver 88, forty years older than he is,
can still work the fields his grandfather cleared,

though he takes it easy on her now,
running his younger Deutz-Allis
to do the heavy work.

When somebody starts up a 39 Gibson
a crowd gathers to listen to the putt-putt
of the single cylinder, as the owner throttles back

until it's barely running, each pop of the engine
puffing a perfect black smoke ring
out of the vertical exhaust.

Women gather at the edge of the dusty field
to renew acquaintances, pass around pictures
of new grand babies and swap casserole recipes.

Each year the men in their feed caps
show a little more curve in their backs,
grow more hair in their ears,

move with less freedom in their rusted joints,
but their machines shine in coats of fresh paint,
a chorus line of pretty, dolled-up floozies.

Casting Call

It was in the papers. They're looking for extras
for a crime thriller they're shooting in Detroit.
It doesn't say exactly what they are looking for
but I think I would be good as *Older Man
Eating Alone* at a restaurant in Greek Town
where Ben Affleck and Matt Damon
are making plans we all know will go awry.

If I wear what I have on today, they might want me
for *Bum Slumped Against Liquor Store*
at Cass and Michigan, drunk on Mad Dog, oblivious
to the car chase with gunfire as it roars past.

I think I'd be perfect as *Curious Onlooker In Crowd*
standing behind yellow crime scene tape
at Rosa Parks and Grand River
sandwiched between *Nosy Woman With Unruly Red Hair*
and *Boy In Hoodie With Skate Board.*

Distinguished Looking Gentleman With Cane
hailing a cab at Woodward and John R?
That might be a stretch for me but I could pull it off
with a little help from wardrobe
and a decent haircut from a Hollywood stylist.
I'm a versatile actor who can play any role
if it's small enough.

The Last Cave Man

He'd spent the morning finishing a mural
of a herd of antelope on the back wall of the cave,
his definitive masterpiece, signing it with a hand print
of oxides that he blew through a hollow reed.

The fire had gone out during the night.
He dreaded spending a whole afternoon
getting it going again, thanks to the dampness
of the fire wood that was left
and the loss of his best piece of flint.

Days ago (there was no number for how many)
his mate had disappeared.
She went down to the river for a gourd of water
and never came back. Probably
those damned hyenas again.

He thought maybe it was time
to consider moving in with the clan
that had built a village in the valley below,
but he couldn't see himself being happy
in a tiny room among other Cro-Magnon
who've grown too old to feed themselves.

Tuesday

On Tuesday the clock in the kitchen stopped.
I can't remember the last time I put a battery in it,
but I'm sure it was more than a year ago.
Imagine a year packed into a single AA battery.

I thought this time I'd leave well enough alone,
let it always be Tuesday at 6:34,
just minutes before the lasagna
comes out of the oven.

Shoveling Snow with Robert Frost

His shoulders were broad
as if the weight of the world
would be no more trouble for him
than a sack of flour would be to you or me.

His hair had not yet turned pure white
and his face lacked the distinctively bushy eyebrows
that would make him instantly recognizable
later in his life.

His hands were paw-like,
red, rough and calloused from years
of manual farm work and piling rocks
at the edges of fields.

"I don't know, Bob. Maybe we should wait;
then when it stops we can get it all."
He shrugged me off and started pulling on
his heavy boots over a pair of thick wool socks.
"We may as well get started," he said.
"It'll just get heavier if we wait."

I was pretty sure that he would be doing
the bulk of the work. His powerful body
seemed better built for it than mine.

"Too bad we're in this subdivision," I said.
"If we were out in somebody's woods
we could just watch them fill up with snow."
"Very funny," he said. "Hand me my gloves
and the red hat with the ear flaps."

First Snow

It arrived early this year,
a week before Thanksgiving
and heavier, I think,
than we have ever seen.
The ground was still warm,
of course, so it began melting
even before it stopped falling.

The fort in the park rose one day
and fell the next, like the walls of Jericho.
The snowman in the neighbor's yard
walked off sometime during the night,
leaving only his ragged, knitted scarf behind.

Niagara Winter

The famous mist had frozen to everything
so solidly that it couldn't be scraped away
so we sat hunkered inside the car,
shivering with the dampness,
listening to Sarah Vaughn, waiting
for the defrosters to do their work,
talking about the drive ahead
over the Rainbow Bridge into New York
and on to Connecticut,
how we thought the little motel in Ontario
was overpriced for this time of year
until we realized the price was in Canadian dollars,
and how the mist, frozen to your eyelashes,
made you look like a chorus girl—
even at this age.

Marginalia

I picture her with red hair in a long braid, freckled nose
and lopsided grin, the way Norman Rockwell might have painted
    her
as a skinny fourteen-year-old uncertain what to do with limbs
that are suddenly too long for her to manage with any sort of grace.

Her name was Beatrice. This much I know from the inside cover of
The Pocket Book of Robert Frost Poems,
for which she'd paid thirty-five cents in 1959,
annotated originally by Luis Untermeyer and later by Beatrice
    herself.

She began on page sixteen with *The Pasture*
where she wrote in the margin with a soft lead pencil,
"I love to rake leaves."
She then skipped over *Home Burial,*
perhaps worried by the darkness of Mr. Frost's theme.

On page forty-seven, *Ghost House,* Beatrice notes
how she loved the image of the ruined fence
and I thought to myself, "So do I, Beatrice. So do I."

A Patch of Old Snow appealed to Beatrice.
She gave it a glowing review.
"I love this poem," she wrote,
"even though I hate litter."

Finally, of *Stopping By Woods on a Snowy Evening,*
all Beatrice had to say to me fifty years in her future was,
"I really wish I could have a horse."

Protective Coloration

The Walking Stick is indistinguishable from his habitat,
as is the Dead Leaf Butterfly, the Pygmy Seahorse,
the Tawny Frog-mouth of Tasmania and the Giant Kelp-fish.

So it is with the poet of a certain age, hidden in a corner booth
at the back of the cafe, as quiet as any snowshoe hare,
as still as a heron among the reeds.

Rust

For as long as I can remember
I have been in love with it,
the gritty feel, sharp smell, rich color.
The square nail that came to daylight
when I turned the garden,
the bloody lines that mark the meridians
of the upturned bowl of a silo's metal roof,
the rivulet of stain that drips
from the "Live Bait" sign
on the crumbling shack at the corner
where we used to turn
to go down to the river,
the Farmall tractor, and the hay rake
it pulled, that sit idle in a field
on an abandoned farm north of town,
the eerie shell of the 39 DeSoto
that, for years, sat on rotting tires
in a patch of weeds behind the butcher shop
before the town itself,
emptied of people and progress,
gradually rusted away.

Ichnology

They left their bare footprints
in what was then wet volcanic ash,
now hardened into crystalline igneous tuff,
several individuals of varying size
headed away from danger.

Along their switchback route
one member stumbles, knees and hands
press into a dark slurry of soft ash.
A larger set of prints turns back,
The pair resumes the journey,
walking with a shortened stride.

Spring Training

They have no idea of their beauty
as they run past the stadium
and round the corner toward the arena,
heading east into the rising sun
through puddled remnants of melting snow.

The leaders are strung out single file
ahead of the pack, stragglers running in pairs
falling farther and farther behind,
ponytails floating behind them
like the long flowing tails of wild mustangs;
chestnut, brindle, black, roan and palomino.

Ex Libris

The noise of pages turning in the library is deafening
despite signs everywhere demanding silence.
The romance section is filled with non-stop sighs
of the starved-for-love and sweet smell of jasmine.

From mysteries there is the crack
of a revolver and from behind a shelf
a woman screams.

Travel is a cacophony of train whistles
boat horns, jet engine sounds,
jangle of busy porters,
people in a hurry.

From history, the sound of clashing swords,
acrid smells of black powder, flashes
of heavy artillery beyond the horizon
like heat lightning, horses in the throes of death,
mourning cries of widows.

In religion, calls to prayer,
odor of brimstone,
moans of the damned.

But in poetry, where both
love and death have come to read,
only the sound of leaves
falling on water.

Lost

Sign on a telephone pole:
Lost Dog, Mixed breed,
some kind of retriever and maybe spaniel.
Blue collar, shaggy black coat,
grizzled muzzle, ears long but not too long,
friendly but shy. Answers to Oswald.

On my way to the bus I watch for him,
any sign of movement in the park or alleys
as I walk by. I wonder of Oswald,
what he was thinking, leaving people who love him,
feed him kibble in a bowl on the floor,
give him his heart-worm pills, clip his nails,
brush his fur, share bites of sandwich under the table.
To lose these things, Oswald must realize,
is the cost of freedom.

Later on the bus I notice
an odd looking man in a baggy suit.
He has shaggy black hair, grizzled face,
the collar of his blue shirt buttoned to the chin.
His ears are long but not too long.
He seems worried and aloof.

"Oswald?" He pretends not to hear me.
Instead, he turns away and puts his head
out of the window, sniffing freedom
through his large, sensitive nose.

Ursa Major and Ursa Minor

There was a first time that someone noticed,
looking into the northern sky,
not one, but two bears
and thought *how ferocious
the stars must be.*

Allegro

Vivaldi's *The Four Seasons* plays in the background
at Peet's Coffee and Tea
where I glance over the shoulder of a stranger
at cryptic lines of mathematical formulae.

Elegant numbers, letters and symbols
fill his computer's glowing screen,
some enclosed in their protective shells of parentheses.

I say to him that they look intimidating
but he tells me that to him they are art
more beautiful than the Mona Lisa,
more spiritual than the ceiling of the Sistine Chapel.

I cannot dispute his claim
and I imagine that I am looking
at the complex equation that explains
life's place in the universe
where Epsilon represents the axial tilt of The Earth,

Lambda, the cosmological constant,
Phi, the golden ratio of art,
Theta, the passage of time,
Sigma, the sum of all things.

The pizzicato notes of *The Winter Concerto*
call to mind the sound of the rain
as it strikes the window and freezes,
at the tempo of both Allegro and Omega.

Wading in Lake Michigan

Each wave you face is the same
and each one different.
The same in how it looks,
the whiteness of its crest,
the deep cerulean of its shadow.
Different in where it breaks on the body,
one just below the knee,
the next just above,
sending an unexpected joy
of cold shock through the groin
and into the brain,
causing you to lift your weight
onto the balls of your feet,
making it feel as if you are lighter.
There is a sudden intake of air to fill lungs
which have become suddenly larger.

Up North

This is where *the north begins*
and the pure waters flow,
if you can believe the motto
underneath the sign proclaiming
that you have just crossed into
the village limits.

If you'd been here a month ago
you could have celebrated both
founders' day and the annual trout festival.
The banner is still up over main street
in front of the court house.

But that was then and this is now
and, as you can see from the sign
on the big church at the other end of town,
it's not too late to attend the annual gun show
and that *Jesus is King of Kings*
and Lord of Lords.

Flemish Painters

A shining pewter bowl overflows with ripe fruit.
A maid peels an apple, light pouring
thick as water through an open window.
A girl reads a book by candlelight, the lids of her eyes
heavy with dreams of exotic countries,
dense jungles and smoky mountains.
A dog lies waiting at the foot of a prince.
A pearl glowing with inner light dangles
below the delicate ear of a young woman.
Tell me van Eyck, de Hooch, Fabritius, Vermeer.
What happens after the light has dimmed,
when the fruit has gone to rot,
the apple has been eaten,
the book has been closed,
the candle blown out,
when the dog has been fed
and the young woman
is no longer young?

1915

If she were alive today
she would have been a hundred,
born into a family that didn't own a radio,
went to bed at dark, got up at dawn
and spent the time between
trying to survive on what they could grow.

A hundred years bridges the time
from the horse and the Model A
to interstate highways,
from a faltering electric light bulb
to street lamps and neon signs,
from telegraph to internet,
from the Wright brothers
to the International Space Station,
from a war fought to end all wars
to the ones we are still fighting.

Sometime, between all of those,
she claims to have once danced
to Jimmy Dorsey's *Amapola*
with George Herman Ruth.

Figurines of Mary in a Salvation Army Store

One appears to be weeping.
Another smiles sweetly, head bowed,
hands pressed together in silent prayer.

Her dark hair is always covered.
Sometimes she is holding her child.
In one version her grown son's thin body
lies stretched across her lap.

Look closely at one and you'll find
the fingers of one hand broken.
On another, the gold trim of her blue robe
has darkened with age.

On some, her arms are outstretched,
ready to hold a rosary. On others,
the hands are turned palms up
in a gesture that invites you to join her
in the serenity of a private grotto.

How these Marys arrived here is no great mystery.
The children, readying mother's house for sale,
sorted each of them into the pile of things
that none of them really wanted to keep,
but which mother would have considered
too sacred to throw away.

Ashcroft's Junkyard

Chevys, Fords, Pontiacs, Plymouths
sit in the sun smiling rusty, toothless grins,
some with one eye blackened
where a headlight has been punched out.

This is the graveyard
where the joyride comes to an end.
Father no longer hangs his elbow
out of the driver's side window.
Mother's blanket and wicker basket
have been removed from the trunk.

A family of field mice has moved into the muffler
of a Bel Air sedan in blue two-tone.
In the wreckage of a Caprice wagon
the Virgin Mary stands abandoned beneath
a rosary that hangs like Spanish moss
from a darkened rear view mirror
permanently twisted to the night view.

Permission to Land

Her husband was a pilot she explains to me
as I rummage through a box of aeronautical charts
on a long table under the shade of an ancient maple
in the front yard of a tidy yellow house.

They are large when they are unfolded,
interesting to look at, with cryptic symbols
for navigational hazards like radio towers,
electrical power lines and buildings taller than two stories,
all the things a pilot would want to avoid.

She tells me I can have the whole box for five bucks.
How could I resist at that price,
a box of charts identifying all of life's dangers,
magnetic compass deviations
and every radio frequency I would ever need
to request permission to land?

Silver Songs

Silver songs turning sienna skies over dunes again,
winter beach morning dressed in khaki coveralls.
Lone fisherman arrives standing cold-raw-broken,
turning near silence where salmon await.
Evening in half-light, silver songs fade into umber beginnings,
traces of cinnabar on burnt umber sands.
Lone fisherman leaves bent cold-raw-broken,
turning near silence where salmon escaped.

Sleeping in Tuscany

We once lived in a large Victorian house
where we could wander from room to room
as if they were small countries in Europe.
We could be in Holland at breakfast,
find ourselves in Belgium at lunch
and Switzerland before dinner.

I liked to sit at my desk in the afternoon
in a northern province of France,
one that I'd never heard of before,
where I could smell the fragrant grapes
that grew on a broken fence outside the window.

In the evening, after the orange light had faded
and the sun had set into the sea west of the Pas-de-Calais,
we would make the long climb into the Alps,
crossing into Italy and our bedroom in Tuscany,
where we could throw open the window and inhale deeply
the off-shore breezes from Corsica.

Twenty-something Poets in Love

You are not Sylvia Plath
and I am not Charles Bukowski.
Now please take your head out of the oven
so I can heat up this pizza
while you study for your biology final.

When I get home from my evening shift at Subway
I'd like to watch that Bergman film on Netflix
with my hand on your breast.
Then we'll write disturbing eulogies for each other,
drink a pint of vodka and go to bed.

Voyager

For Carl Sagan

The images were spectacular.
The rings of Saturn,
the goddess moons of Jupiter,
the sulfur spewing fires of Io.

They tell us now that it's no longer a part of the solar system,
that it belongs to the stars,
has broken some invisible boundary
of deep time into cosmological forever.

Its radio signal was photographed from Earth
as a pale blue dot, twenty-two watts,
like the light bulb in a refrigerator.
One pale blue dot as seen from another.

Grace Chapel

Wires from a neon sign that once proclaimed,
Jesus Saves, dangle above
the boarded-over front door.

The pastor, who worked days at a grain elevator,
packed up and moved his family to the city years ago
before the last of his congregation died out.

Ragweed and goldenrod have pushed themselves
up through the graveled parking lot where flat-bed trucks
and the occasional tractor would gather
Sunday mornings and Wednesday evenings
for long sermons that floated out through windows
open to the summer air.

The last of them was about forgiveness,
according to a fallen sign that lies on its back
in a patch of stinging nettles
which it wears like a thorny crown.

The Widower

She would have told him
not to eat that. It's been
in the refrigerator too long.

He pauses over the sink,
lifts the lid to give it a sniff
the way she would have done
before throwing it out,
then he opens the drawer
to find a fork.

Anna Karenina at the Beach

Well, at least in the form of her book,
a paperback edition from *Bantam Classics*
with a picture of Anna on the cover
looking remarkably like Keira Knightley,
which I found abandoned on a park bench
overlooking the water.

It was left, I imagine, by a college student
who had good intentions of reading it,
but who was, instead, distracted
by an afternoon volleyball game.

Poor Anna, cover coated with a film
of morning dampness,
pages fluttering in an onshore wind,
alone with a momentous decision to make,
and the railroad station nowhere in sight.

Stanza Means Room in Italian

Il saggiorno (the living room)
with its chesterfield divan,
fireplace chenets, the chaise
perfect for a faint if someone
were to mention bare skin
or the prospect of a dalliance,
etagere along the boiserie wall,
large jardiniere standing in one corner.

La sala da prannzo (the dining room)
with gleaming chandelier,
girandole on the credenza, the long buffet,
rows of straight backed chairs
at the cabriolet legged table
on intaglio marble floor.

La camera da letto (the bedroom)
with its arabesque armoire,
boulle jewel box on the breakfront,
fauteuil in a corner of the room
in front of a carefully suspended beauvais
and the carlton holding the veilleuse.

La cucina (the kitchen)
with its Frigidaire, Hotpoint,
Sunbeam, Kenmore.

Eye Exam

It always begins with the letter E
which is so large on the chart
that I should be able to read it in the mountains
from the floor of the valley below.

The F and the P on the second line
are just a little bit smaller,
still not much of a challenge.

By the third line
myopia begins to take its toll
and I wonder, perhaps out loud,
if T O Z isn't a word.

Line four, I'm pretty sure,
contains a reference
to the Los Angeles Police Department,

The next line is guess at best,
the first letter being a C and O or a G.
There's no way to tell for sure.

Below that are what appear to several lines
that were written by an unknown Russian poet.
This I can tell from the sadness
of the few letters I am able to read.

A Sharpshooter's Last Sleep

After a photograph by Alexander Gardner:
—Gettysburg, Pennsylvania—July 4, 1863

He lies on a mattress of hard earth
as if he has fallen asleep, one knee bent,
arms resting comfortably by his side
the way he might have lain at home in his own bed.

Leaves of a mulberry stir in the morning breeze.
The sounds of battle have faded but
traces of black powder smoke sour the air.

If I could kneel down with my ear close to his,
I might hear his mother's voice
calling him to morning chores before breakfast,
a call that will not rouse him today.

Jesus of Ypsilanti

Reuben came home from the state institution
declaring that he was no longer Jesus.
It came as a great relief to all of us
who found Jesus to be an annoying man,
ragged, blunt in his speech and rarely showered.
I sometimes missed him, but even more,
I missed the wine that he swore had once been water.

How to Fly

The book is like a pair of opened wings
on the round kitchen table.
It has the same title as this poem.
Some of the illustrations are in color,
charts and graphs mostly black and white.

There is a table of contents at the front,
a glossary of terms at the back.
The chapters have titles like
Basic Principles of Aerodynamics,
Reducing Drag and, my favorite, *Generating Lift.*

Outside the window a pair of mourning doves
is raising two chicks in a nest under the eaves.
I sit at the table with my cup of tea,
turn to the chapter on *Takeoffs and Landings,*
begin reading to them aloud.

Dark City

Dark City is a mighty beast,
a sprawling monster
with a skeleton of steel
covered in a concrete overcoat.

In Dark City laws and souls
are trampled in the street.
The strong eat the weak.
Lives dangle from dangerous heights.

Living here is a fevered dream.
A man can go off his nut on these streets
among the jaundiced cops,
corrupt politicians, psychotic crooks.

In the city's tenderloin the seedy rooms
are clammy with the residue
of spoiled hopes, abandoned dreams,
wallpaper that sweats fear.

Everywhere is the crackle and buzz
of neon signs that stare each other down
across dirty streets
and grimy infected avenues.

Dark City is a mighty beast
with a taste for human flesh,
your flesh if you make a wrong turn.
That bullet in your forehead
was meant to slow you down.

Mr. Big

Harry the Horse says,
"The Boss wants to see you."
Ordinarily I'd decline his invitation
but he's got his hand in his coat pocket
and something in it is pointed at my chest.

Everybody wants to see Mr. Big
when they want to see him.
Nobody wants to see Mr. Big
when he wants to see them.

He's the pope of the city.
Everybody kisses the big diamond he wears
on the manicured pinky of his right hand.

From his office in the back of the nightclub
Mr. Big runs the dark side of the city.
He owns the mayor, the chief of police,
most of the city council,
even fifty percent of the governor.

He understands that anyone
who is his friend is also his enemy,
that loyalty walks a tight-wire
stretched between greed and fear.

He's Genghis Khan, Alexander,
Napoleon, Caesar, and Ivan the Terrible
ground up and rolled into one fat little sausage.
Just one of those gigantic cigars that he smokes
is worth more than your life.

Gorillas

We don't know what their mothers called them.
We know them by handles like Whitey,
Slim, Shorty, Bugs, Mugsy and Rocky.
Two of them are permanently on guard
outside Mr. Big's office door
in the back of the night club.

One of them chews on a toothpick.
The other tosses a silver dollar
over and over, always coming up heads.

They're mugs, henchmen, hoodlums,
goons, gorillas, muscle,
hoods in black fedoras.

They want to take you for a ride
but not before they've broken
a few of your ribs.

They're a couple of empty suits,
afraid of nothing except for their
hat-check-girl and dime-a-dance girlfriends.

Don't Forget Your Hat

When you need to know who's who and what's what
in this town, get to know the hat check girl at Mr. Big's.
She rubs elbows with the best and the worst:
the millionaire bankers and street thugs,
the gamblers, gangsters and high society wags,
the artsy set, the Hollywood stars,
the phony tipsters and juggernauts of Wall Street.

She knows them all and she knows their business.
She's a friendly small town girl
from one of those states that begins with an *I*.
She came to the city to be a dancer.
but all she found were a lot of bright lights
and empty promises. She took the only work she could get.
It barely pays the bills but she'll be okay
because surviving here is all about what you know
and, believe me, she knows plenty.

Don't fall for that simple country girl act.
That's just her way of seeming harmless.
And don't ever give her the double-cross.
The dame's got friends—if you know what I mean.

The Dark

As many things exist in the dark
as do in the light
and, who knows, maybe more.
It is the possible discrepancy
that worries us.

Hyde

Perhaps you prefer a gentleman. One of those
panting hypocrites who like your legs but talk
about your garters.
       —Fredric March as Mr. Hyde (1931)

To be perfectly honest,
I haven't been feeling myself lately.
Doctor Jekyll hasn't made a diagnosis
but he's trying different medications
hoping some combination of them will help.

I can describe the worst of the symptoms.
People say I've been irritable.
I wake up mornings soaked in sweat.
I find hair growing in the oddest places.

My girlfriend says she doesn't know me.
People who should recognize me
act like they've never seen me before.
I've been tired during the day like I haven't slept.

Tonight I'm locking myself in.
I've heard a rumor that some of my friends
are planning an intervention
but I swear everything I take is by prescription.

Wrong Turn on Scarlet Street

It's easy in a strange neighborhood
in the night city to make that one wrong turn
onto a narrow street
you've never been down before.

Life is like that sometimes.
One minute you're at a party
honoring your twenty-five years of service
to mediocrity and boredom.

The next minute you're lost
and looking for a way back home.
But there is no way back home
once you've made that wrong turn.

You realize somewhere along the way
you've grown old and ugly,
that your life is a prison,
your own conscience, the warden.

Then comes that one night
you see a chance to bust out
so you take it, and from there
fate drags you down that evil street.

Once you've sold your life and your soul
you can never buy them back
even if you can steal enough to afford them.
All sales are final on Scarlet Street.

Death by Poison

I love the way this poem starts out
at the farthest end of a long curving gravel drive
lined with ancient elms that leads to a manor house.
And I especially love that no rain is expected
before the fourth stanza.

The Edwardians were so refined,
unlike like the Victorians for whom the sun
never seemed to shine
and who took everything so seriously.

And unlike the Elizabethans
in their oh so uncomfortable clothes,
and those smirky looks about what really
lay underneath all those codpieces.

I prefer the Edwardians in their formal gardens,
playing croquet on manicured lawns,
gin and tonics in their hands.
Now comes that rain, right on schedule,
meaning old Lord Carrington is about to die
a horrible death by poison.

To Have and Have Not

In the balcony rows where the lovers sit
it's not so far from heaven
where the beam from a projector
slices the darkness and we,
playing at Bogie and Bacall,
splash ourselves up on the screen,
an etching of a former world,
where we wish we could
live out our lives in two dimensions
in the deep shadows of a darkened theater,
the objects of every envy.

About the Author

David Jibson grew up in rural Michigan. He is retired from a forty year career as a social worker, most recently with a hospice agency. He is a graduate of Western Michigan University in Interdisciplinary Communications and of Michigan State University, M.S.W. Currently he is co-editor of Third Wednesday Magazine, a quarterly print journal of literary and visual art, and a coordinator of events for The Crazy Wisdom Poetry Circle in Ann Arbor, the place he now calls home.

www.ingramcontent.com/pod-product-compliance
Lightning Source LLC
Chambersburg PA
CBHW022202080426
42734CB00006B/546